Idiopaths

poems by

Bill Rasmovicz

Brooklyn Arts Press · New York

Idiopaths
© 2014 Bill Rasmovicz

ISBN-13: 978-1-936767-21-2

Cover design by Kelley Erickson. Book design by Joe Pan.

All Rights Reserved. No part of this publication may be
reproduced by any means existing or to be developed
in the future without the written consent of the publisher.

Published in the United States of America by:
Brooklyn Arts Press
154 N 9th St #1
Brooklyn, NY 11249
www.BrooklynArtsPress.com
info@brooklynartspress.com

Distributed to the trade by Small Press Distribution / SPD
www.spdbooks.org

Library of Congress Cataloging-in-Publication Data

Rasmovicz, Bill, 1970-
 [Poems. Selections]
 Idiopaths / by Bill Rasmovicz.
    pages ; cm.
 ISBN 978-1-936767-21-2 (pbk. : alk. paper)
 I. Title.

 PS3618.A77I34 2013
 811'.6--dc23

                                        2013004199
10 9 8 7 6 5 4 3 2 1
FIRST EDITION

CONTENTS

I. Sundays in the Foreign Country of Kindness

clear smoke / 13

telephone number to a bomb / 14

we were the manifestation of a splayed rainbow / 15

after effects / 16

sundays in the foreign country of kindness / 17

examination room / 18

hieroglyphics of ache / 20

wrath / 21

the black pill of childhood / 22

one bullet is a full chamber / 23

II. The Resurrection Machine Mauve

the resurrection machine mauve / 26

III. The Empire of Absinthe

the man who looked like an angel who looked like a man / 36

smokestacks / 37

dawn through the fuselage / 38

the empire of absinthe / 43

slow lives of the statues / 44

distillates of another evening wasted / 46

amidst the eternity of when you told me / i thought you were you, / and then i thought you weren't / 48

the sum of things less than their parts / 49

IV. Via Negativa

via negativa / 52

About the Poet

Idiopaths

I.
Sundays in the Foreign Country of Kindness

CLEAR SMOKE

I believe in the conquest of ants, the metal-tearing
claw end of a hammer, anything discerned
with your teeth, a pear, a screw

that afterwards the angel deep throats its trumpet
that in the artifice of the body we are small, so small

I believe in painting the fire escape the color of water
that the starling's center is a single rusted nail
afternoons clear smoke

in the exhaustion of pastured cows
to cement this whole scene down, the confusion
of cop cars around the missing appendage washed ashore

that if you ask a quivering leaf its address it will reply
with a more amplified quiver

the river will not forget your name, it never knew it
we are conceived in the forest softly as ferns

TELEPHONE NUMBER TO A BOMB

My father was a shaman in hunter orange igniting the woods.
My mother persisted on buttered toast
and cigarettes. I was her little son-of-a-bitch upstairs somewhere

pissing out a window, firing arrows into the paneling.
Our phone number was a bomb's, [1(0 9 8)-7 6 5- 4 3 2 1].
Horns grew from the walls. Cheap whiskey lay trophied in crystal

on dovetailed mahogany. Inside the psyche
it was all grey teats for clouds, knives under the bed. I, blithe
idiopath whose daydream cathedral was toxic neon

stars plastered to the ceiling, picking hellgrammites under
river rocks. No one could account for my sister's extra kidney,
her having been born via the coal chute, waifish,

almost immaterial. All I wanted was to be instrumental as needle-
nose pliers, purposed in wrongdoing as a tattoo on the throat.

WE WERE THE MANIFESTATION
OF A SPLAYED RAINBOW

Grandfather hacked his lungs into the yard.
Pears absorbed the yellow jackets.

We were our own souvenirs for having survived.
Pigs' feet lay suspended in jelly, unaware

their weight would tear the cupboards from the wall
while the electrical tower loomed over us,

a mute dictator. Evenings, we listened for
the acid-talk of coyotes on the hillside, wagering

if a soup bone would coax oblivion
from its den beneath the porch. Crows knew

your name. Memory thinned to erasure
under acetone stars. Ashes settled on your sleep.

AFTER EFFECTS

After they wheeled you out, quadruple-dosed, a wet leaf.
After the blackout and the neighborhood gone missing.

After hair grew in the corners of the rooms.
After the earthworm broke in two and writhed, a talisman in the palm.

After the foxes' eyes reflecting the spotlight back, double bright,
the trees asphyxiated in moth-web.

After the barbed-wire threshold and man standing there at trigger,
grass cuts in the corners of his mouth.

After slipping the cigarette over the fuse to delay the explosion.
After the stench of hospital in your clothes.

After the skull with its one horn strung across the driveway
through the eye sockets, rubbing holes in the skin with an eraser.

Further, way past the street's dead end,
after the robin's yolk under the fingernails—
one horse, two sweetened gas tanks, four windshields later—

SUNDAYS IN THE FOREIGN COUNTRY OF KINDNESS

The low branch of the thorn tree cocked
is a weapon. Mind, a nest of trip-wires.

Geese vaporized through the jet's turbines
are just another form of air.

Night-long the television stays on, a pill
inducing sleep. Its characters

like cells of your blood viewed through
a microscope, tiny directionless clouds.

EXAMINATION ROOM

Boy w/Residual Antler

Is your inner voice helium-infused?
Is the cage of your chest a crime scene
where one bird has murdered the other?

Does your spirit leave a wake?
Does a plum-eyed steed harass you in your sleep?

Which is more feral against you, moonglow or the torn
edge of sheet metal?

Have you ever felt an animal separated from its skin?
Do you find the goldfinch's colors narcotic?

Feel lighter by each breath? Stuffed
with horsehair and springs?

Can you auscultate the slow pulse of an oak
with your palm?

Do you hear the grasses moan when a mushroom
is plucked from the earth?

Boy w/Horsehead

Is the air a silverfish on your cheek?
Do the leaves sound like
exterior panic?

When you wake, is it bilge you taste,
lead pencil shavings, scorched barnwood?

Is your pulse dimmer than a
junkyard séance? Does your dewclaw
tangle in the wind's black hair?

Is it the fat of the animal you crave,
or the aura after the shot?

HIEROGLYPHICS OF ACHE

I was running, nowhere and shirtless, the sky Valium blue.
Addle-headed, I tripped, descending the slope of raw wheat-like

grasses face-first into summer. When I arose,
the brush burn over my left nipple was a nervy radiance

in complete opposition to the afternoon's foofy clouds
and fattened bees. The garage was emphysemic, sucked

into itself. Water bugs treaded rainwater in a brackish tub.
There was an austerity to the sun's brightness, equal and opposite

my squinting, like this wound where there was already a scar
just seemingly for having been.

WRATH

This is to say that when the floodwater abated,
the bridge never tore away completely, but lay limp

a full year after, like a mink's leg in the trap,
that over a summer of scratching itself hairless,
its inflammations turned black

and the cat never came around anymore.
This is about the wasp in the lock of the front door,

the house at night setting its break or breaking,
the purpled sidewalk this morning after rain

pelted the lilac into a weird ecstasy of hurt.
How when sister Liguori whipped her fat hand across

that kid's face, immediately it was known there was
remittance for nothing ever purchased or received.

That anyone could live so long on translucent tubes
and the machined beeps of a truck backing up.

That the clavicle was never a bow against
the instrument of the sky, and the skull with its vacant

eyes too heavy for the dining room wall remains
the trophy around which we still gather and eat.

THE BLACK PILL OF CHILDHOOD

I cased the place. I mean
I cased the place, paced to where my heels
bludgeoned the road like the butts of rifles.

I hollered for anyone's attention. Nope.
Looked both ways twice,
then pitched my assault and smashed every window
of that attorney's vacation house.

I knelt down, drew my blade, and eviscerated the evening.
The art and the facts
left for someone else to piece together later.

The clouds, conjugated tire smoke.
The limp hillside with its lung brushes for trees.

I knew then I would stir my coffee with an ice pick
when I grew up, that I would find a way
to sell this goddamn pantomiming sunset if I could.

ONE BULLET IS A FULL CHAMBER

Amidst the austerity of copulating branches
and freezing delirium, if not almost asleep,
I let the spiker wander in perfect range, two doe trailing.
It glanced my way, then lowered its nose

to the leaves. Scientifically, I placed the x and y horse hair
axes on its shoulder and watched it collapse into
itself, overcome by a fantastic rapture, like the disciples

on TV when the preacher palm-punched their foreheads.
When my father opened the animal, the entrails
steamed into a vortex of malodor. Then his reaching

high in its cavity for the heart, the fleas of its spattered
coat banging about. Then cutting off the scent sacks
and word that next time I would do the dressing.

I stood at the shore of my mind's chrome lake
deciding how to cross in winter clothes. No feeling

sorry, simply the clunky ownership
of dragging it two hours from the woods, tongue
dumb and spilling from its mouth, eyes
wide, still searching for something to fill its hunger.

II.
The Resurrection Machine Mauve

THE RESURRECTION MACHINE MAUVE

What might have ruined me, that I became;
an erratic, complicated shape, like a tool
for some obsolete task.

Evening arrives
and I feel myself in the threshold of my face.

Outside, in the gutter beside the sidewalk, the crow
struts back and forth,
the air becoming air becoming no air again.

In a city complicated by ruin and dialect, I came to my senses
with a pencil in my hand.

How quiet chaos is. How tracelessly it enters the books
that fill the room.
Even my handwriting is lonely.

The human body is not the world, and yet it is; the undersides
paler than a torn Japanese umbrella.

The mornings pass clear and deserted.
Fueled by ether and paradox, I stagger out of bed
like a scarecrow pulled into halves.

I graze on the barbed hook,
the invisible life that sleeps in the grossness of things.

I am not sure there is a cure—
every day now chill and a glaze.

I'd have thought by now it would have stopped.

But I have to smile, whatever the winter; I belong here.
I was born, the blueness of the hour
misting in,

violet snow in the window, merely wanting words.

The room has three suitcases.
My beard is thick, my eyelids half cover
the walls, the curtains.

I am a moth of sorts, the way I strip down
invisible to others, this light I subscribe to.
I keep a worn-out owl around.

Here it is again, the old humiliation
with its dull, dark, unutterable rigor. Can you imagine the air
filled with smoke
like an old memory gradually changing into you?

After the adaptable man and the man pierced through,
I return,
a certain traveler who believed in nothing.

Mosquitoes stick to the wet paint.
I wonder who has pissed here.
Outside, a man roams the streets with a basket.
Of course the day doesn't tremble, not visibly. And houses,
however neighborly to the eye, house discomfort.

How many times in cold and fog I've waited,
lean, straight as a weapon.
I thought my life was always incurable, endless.

I look around in the unknown year, aware that few
are a model for modern angels.

The half-open window frames a face:
beyond the hallways and windows shadowed by neglect,
I contemplate my burial and resurrection
into a puddle of sleep.

These days, I wake in the used light in the corner
of the attic, the clock
straining to pull me out of my body
while the curtain's gauze is a nurse across the floor.

I have not handled the ordinary well.
Today things are the coffins of remembrance; this sudden
and tiny shower, stage-lit streets.
At the remains of one who took on such light

Often I stand in the yard with a shovel, useless.
Sometimes I walk down the street
eating clouds. When no one's watching

I kneel down and practice my howling.
This is the creature I am: on my skin, this wretched fever.
Can't you still smell the smoke on my body?

I had thought it would be different.

Moss grows in the shadows of the square.
At six every night the women sit in chairs, my tallness
less to them than a pillar of salt.
Their faces tell there is a hell and they will reach it.

And isn't the body a tangled garden no one can leave?
How have I lived here so long?
Behind the house is a leaky saucepan of destinies
where a branch once held
the tree trembling in place, I know it's all not real—

Wherever I go, it's there, fog heaved in like a headache,
only more ambitious.

All my life I felt the gradual wearing away leaves us alive.
In the principalities of my own gaze, some grief
is larger than my body is.

Birds leave their shadows.
Chimneys salute this departure with smoke.

I live in a glove shop.
Each night's a liberation. You see light reflecting
scattered with the crunching fingers of gods and Caesars.

Rivers grow small. Cities grow small. And splendid gardens
forget about us.

To laugh and look through the crowd as it passes
at the exact center of the modern world, a mob of people
with blank faces.

In the middle of the night I ask myself:
why was I not simply born in the grass?

Man flees suffocation.
The ponderous barges push their way slowly upriver
like wolves ennobled.

We keep on building the empire, and before you notice,
it's become an abyss.

The wind slashes its own face.
My shadow stretches over the street on the burning asphalt.
And now soldiers, darkness, prayers.
A melancholy stationmaster withers in a prison cell.

We learn in the retreating, this world is not conclusion.
Having tried hope,
I'll wander these streets until I'm dead tired.

On foot, theoretically alive, I imagine I am moving on.

I am on a large iron bird sailing past death.

Here's what I see: shapes as a series of edges,
nothing at all except the stubbornness
of things.

I lie beneath the stars of another sky.
All ideas escape me.

Within my reach, time present and time past,
pouring its soft light down on all the secret houses.

I can hear everything:
the history of strangers in their dreams, and toward evening,
the empty bell.

I do not know much about the gods, but I think that the river
is the color which night decomposes.
And down the street they are pulverizing
the old wilderness.

Is what one sees always sweetness and horror fused
in a single music?

The drunk mechanic is happy to be in the ditch.
The hospital pursues its daily ration.

There is no prophecy, only memory.
Uncertain, alone,
I see an earth that is already extinguished.

Inside me, the shadows are articulate
although they will not speak: it's the sort of weather
Tybalt murdered Mercutio in, this great liquid silence.

A clothesline swings from the house.
Serenity lopes along like exhaustion, slack-jawed
in burning cold.

It is all so pitiful, really. The little photographs hang
on the pallid wall. We hardly ever see the moon anymore.

Imagine the clock—from the bones of animals, windows
no one has ever looked out of.

In this country, only the dead can be born again,
and then not much.

At night your mouth bleeds. The day is too bright,
while the child with wild red hair runs away, or is lost in the light.

III.
The Empire of Absinthe

THE MAN WHO LOOKED LIKE AN ANGEL WHO LOOKED LIKE A MAN

These wings, each one with its own itinerary and
compass, incongruous with what the body's heft requires.

They indict one another with lassitude or obstinacy, not
in the glassy subterfuge of voice—a banter under the guise
of garbage men clunking cans in the twilight dawn—

but something visible, if you could see them,

in the botched exchange of their flagellations,
or as steam evanescing
through the grated sidewalks, where,
upon a gust of wind, I witnessed a man fall from

the curb, and without ever using his arms to brace himself,
leave his teeth in the street.

SMOKESTACKS

Dead as they are they remain, almost Roman,
testaments to the wherewithal of concrete,
mange of an idea. Now smoke rises from the ground.

If you wander up the hillside you can put your
hand over the vents where it steams, scorched

earth, rich and sulfuric. Over the valley
of inconsolable buildings, the river wedging
itself between waste and wasted, you feel ashen,

a gone-broke soap opera star, or an astro-monkey
experimented upon, retired-from-science, deranged,
criminal: the urge to annihilate yourself, luxuriously.

DAWN THROUGH THE FUSELAGE

Rose petals in a black bowl. The foreign country of a kiss.
O richness of memory,

raft of splintered wood and empty barrels.
O curvature of the spine, architecturally disfigured
but still load-bearing.
O empire of it forever being after midnight on the body clock
in the middle of the afternoon, of ubiquitous tip jars
and shoes the addictive consistency of pot roast.

Each morning a man maims the same tune on the subway platform.
Concierge half asleep in your chair, do you half-hear, half-see
the silverfish?

The hour decomposes around a dove clasping its branch.
The tree plucking its feathers out,

beneath which, a woman whose child cares nothing
for the world at large, saying *Shit! Shit!*
and never remembering any of it.

Body, where is your locus, your infinitely collapsed
center beyond which not even light escapes?

Mass grave, receipt from the purchase of the family plot.
O sticking the butter knife in the socket for the shock.

Tiny vortex trailing a raindrop,
replica of the masterpiece too valuable to exhibit,
we are just like you, all front facade, attitude till hurt ensues.

Shrapnel seeking soft tissue, is our desire not
the same? Lost balloon we know your message is
I'm not coming back.

Bong water, scat in a paper bag aflame on our porch.
O holy prank of the skin in which we reside.

I am convinced:

The occupants upstairs will continue their pursuit late night
via power tools.

Of the divining sway of the buzzard's blood-red wattle.
That the shaman's jewelry, teeth, and wardrobe are all that remains.

That the wood bee will return one August afternoon to a hive
caulked and painted over.
Of the hole in the skull while the patient remains awake.

That whatever animal it is at 3 AM
beneath the living room floorboards is more at home.

Of the tiny hammer in the alarm,
the strength-to-weight ratio of the nest wedged between rafters
propping up the roof propping up the sky.

The weatherman with his mason's teeth and mercenary's smile.

The streetlamp with its malarial hue.
The resolution of the bell to pull down the tower.

That until you've drank from the vivisected head of the plastic baby doll
found at shoreline

will you understand half of what a dandelion root knows,
can you come to your name as your own.

When I eyed the rifle's steel bead to the bluebird and pulsed
its quarter moon trigger, the next scene
was me standing over it as it thrashed in the dirt, color

bleeding into atmosphere. Amazed how concentration
nullified dimension, that a valence of
who I was vanished, too, a bird the color of sky.

And with my father, ascending the alley toward ambulance lights,
uniforms escorting from the falling-down house

its inhabitant, injury-drunk, the fruit of his face pummeled to
pink distortion. Sumac alchemical amidst the panic-lights

where the urge still lingered to fuse face and bat
into one blunt object.
His stumble into me bloodying my shirt.

A worm grinding across red bricks—*that* is morning.

Each second the clock fires its arrow into the brittle
integument of the future,
The warehouse contemplates its barren lot into collapse.

History, the first thing we accrue is dust.
Coefficient of friction, we present
a stain in the street as percentage, a deposit for what's to come.

Adrenaline moon. O cilia and street corner
cordoned by police tape, tungsten sun.

The night relents to make a chord of its solitary voice.
The houses maintain their solemn tenure, their pigeon-torn
rooftops, and lights unanimously out.

THE EMPIRE OF ABSINTHE

All the buildings were smoke-bearded and swayed
wasted on nitrous. Quiet. Though you could hear through

the balls of your feet the muffled intonations of a toy piano
navigating the sewers below. I had a paper cut for a voice.
I was mostly alone. But the aura was a crowd in which I

was to be beaten with the belt of my tongue.
Sky was a pelt stretched steeple to needle-nose steeple.

Just to breathe was to inhale through couch cushions soaked
in gasoline. Half floating, half sitting, a woman bled her

nose into a white rag while her little god routed through
the museum's bushes for the legs of crickets to twist.

SLOW LIVES OF THE STATUES

Pressing my ear to the tracks, the goiter angel
shrieking. In my head, stalactites

dripping all the time. Some days I am tall and
slender as a weapon. Other days my skin
is radiated milk. Numbness occupies my hands.

Often I go to the door and no one is there.
I keep a bowl of rusted keys around,

understand the steam from the rooftops as
nothing less than buildings consuming themselves,

the quiet boring a space within us to fill
or make more hollow. Each morning I wake

to the restaurant emptying its artillery of bottles
into the alley, while evening is the hue

of an apple left atop the radiator. In the alliteration
of streets I think of the woman who never

leaves her home anymore, the reflections
of the city as a city itself, how she seems kin

of an empire burnt and still burning. I too wish
for the slow lives of the statues to catch up,

the analgesic of snow to smother the snow.
I know a tree cracking in the cold is the densest

kind of ache, that there are always the intoxicated
lights of a few cars intent on a barbed
and blacked-out horizon. Swallows nest

in the crumbling smoke stacks. Mistaken
are the cinders falling for feathers and vice versa.

DISTILLATES OF ANOTHER EVENING WASTED

I.

Curbside of busted rims and black snow.
Girl swiped from the grocery store in the news.

Steam bellows from stainless steel
to the fortitude of industry.

The happenstance of happiness, you think.
Dead leaves flagellate the branch.

Hoodlums toss bottles from the back of a car
screaming fuck you to anyone.

Breath on the window or the window itself breathing.
History's mantra, that even a river

can be coaxed to flame.
Words no substitute for the thing itself.

The wind transacts without remainder.
Parking meters flash zeros into the thousandths.

Through the window, a woman whose fingernails
grow only to perpetuate her anxiety.

II.

The shadow of a bird
traversing the shadow of a fire escape.
Never opening its mouth, a siren wails through its teeth.

The concrete side of the hotel weathered
into a 12-story x-ray of a spinal cord.
Ice-melt from the balcony above.

The slits between the ribs, narrow valves to let the light
in, pressure out.

The air's heavy hollow.
The bones heavy, hollow.

The bleached corks of our bodies
making off as passersby below.

AMIDST THE ETERNITY OF WHEN YOU TOLD ME I THOUGHT YOU WERE YOU, AND THEN I THOUGHT YOU WEREN'T

This is the forty-ton statue
of a man on a horse, tribute to the nameless.
Here, a tear in the sky's meniscus,
something sinking.

A radio's rust-coated voice,
smolder from its throat.

An evening borne of fog and sewer light, an evening
turned over on its back, odor of meat.

Here, this looted mosaic
to reflect that the dead
still have to deal with their hair growing,
a nail limp at the door of impenetrable wood.

A heap of clothes on a cobblestoned bridge.
A man performing the Heimlich on his accordion.

A pillar, standing there.
The poppies standing there,
pushing blood-tinged and nightward

from a planet secured to the moon's
umbilicus by its teeth.

THE SUM OF THINGS LESS THAN THEIR PARTS

Trying to discern greatness from greatness
I left the frescoes of Assisi sick of Giotto, hollowed
or filled, I couldn't tell.

I sat down on the wall to eat my sandwich, my neck
stiff from gazing up. The caretaker cutting grass—
nothing but the meditation of duty.

The desiccated high clouds, the valley with its ebullient
greens and blueprint of farms—real things,
but I had given up this world already.

I wandered up the hill for immersion
or erasure. Whose guts, I wondered, were forfeited to
the cobblestones beneath me? Someone's wine

smashed and bled into the street. Water spurted from the
stone mouths of mythological fish. Everywhere was
ice-cream, antennae, outdoor seating. Words

or their absence: I could find neither.
The pillars of old Rome and the hot odor
of dog urine, me the animal waiting for the instant
I could come back to my body.

IV.
VIA NEGATIVA

VIA NEGATIVA

The only thing I remember is that you were
pitch blue,   dormant as the rifles

in the lacquered drawers behind you.

Whatever occupied the body went on without
the body.   That, even I could discern.

A condition like sleep,
but you had passed the border of sleep,
found a break in the fence and kept on

so deep in the trees we would never find you.
That's how I think of it, brother.

Cloudy tomorrow and 53. Cloudy Wednesday
and 60. Periods of sun and 64…

This is what we look forward to.
Not that the predictions are accurate,
or knowing anything about anything
is accurate.

It is a starting point.
With you, there is no starting point.

We begin and begin and begin again.
It complicates us all.

Brother, I think the super predator
is man, how we consume
and consume each other, nothing more than
the myth of ourselves,
our own feral   creations,

that the thought of ourselves is our selves.

And thinking that, I feel phosphorescent,
tentacled   and chartreuse,   adrift in

the center of something that
won't shut off.

It pulses and rests, pulses and rests
like waves pummeling   the shoreline
of a coast wooded and desolate,

or more like wind teasing its fingers through
the horse diamond's oblique grasses.
I can't say how for sure.
But I feel outside myself.

I know the containment of the skin is limiting.
         I've seen how the body
is merely an outline in the street.

It's as though the hair on my arms were
growing coarse, my skin taut,   resilient.

Brother, I feel more animal than ever.

I keep noticing the leaves twitch,
the nervous bodily discourse of prey.

If I passed right here   now
into that forest with you,

I'd dissolve   into dirt or atmosphere
and continue, like you, without mass
or weight.   I know I
would continue.

You are absence, yes,   a hole of sorts,
defined by what
surrounds   you. A zero,

an abstraction. This is the only way
we can know you.
Pythagoras desired to explain the world
in numbers,

as though the coordinates of a place
or a quantity could be   distilled
     to emotion,

sensibility, a mood, a color.

Brother, I feel weird saying it,
but for me, 1 is white, 2 is blue, 3 yellow,
    4 purple, 5 red, 6 blue, 7 gold,

8 black, and 9 sun-colored,

I can't say why.
Like why you can't see the sky in front
of you, only from afar,

or that the barges   weighed with so much
cargo float so easily,
more definitively, upriver.

As if it were an equation
to solve, triangulate our relationship
or lack   to you

via something solid and dimensional
as the room you left, this photograph.

And nothing. There is no tertiary position
from which to gauge.

It's like that barge, the heavier it is
the more water is displaced.

That's what we are to you, a displacement.
The more   we think of you,
the more we are disembodied.

If the ghost of you keeps growing older—
does it grow older?—
I can't conceive what urland you'd inhabit.

The school 23 years empty now?
The factory,   dropping brick by soot-caked
brick   into the river?

At the bottom of the air shaft?
I bet no sunlight reaches
          the bottom of that shaft, brother.

It's inflammatory, this condition.
Thinking perpetuates itself.

A seed falls and immediately
roots again.
And then another
and so on, exponentially

until a vast patch of briars   weeds up,
netting everything.

Or swimming in the sea, the way one feels
intimate with the salt and brine
and necessary minerality,
and absolutely lost, too. Departed, somehow.

For some reason, I don't picture you at the sea.
I imagine   you following the singular runs
of deer, scouting

teaberries, or lazing on a fallen coat
of spruce.

Under that spruce,
I know that if I were cut open   right now
like that deer I put a bullet through,
I too would cover everything in a wash

of chrome all the way to the mountain.

I would remain something glacial, a fixture
of landscape,
         evaporating and precipitating
myself upon myself.

Gone and remaining.

I'm sure now that *when*
is a function of *where*, that time

is a function of place.

We used to go down to the air shaft,
prop a dead tree or mangled car part against
its corroded exterior

and clamber up to the rusted chain link,
the shaft   like a cathedral

we sprawled over
watching mass,
if the dome were transparent,

and mass the rainwater and gunk
alchemizing   at the bottom.

You could hardly see bottom it was so deep.
You could plummet your voice down
and   it would return someone else's,

its acoustics televangelical,
its low-voltage radiance
filling you.

Any junk muffler, dead branch, or rock we
could navigate through the links
     we'd let fall
just to hear that thing swallow.

In that sound, you rethought yourself.
You were afraid for your life
spread-eagled atop its rickety geometry,

a star on a Christmas tree,

compelled.
You became something knifelike,
precise   and purposed, almost
miracled, hearing the earth summon you
in its guttural tongue.

I don't know why, brother, but I can't
remember faces anymore.

I can know   someone and love them, but
as soon as they're gone and I try to
picture their face,

the topography is snow-covered.

It's as if they passed some event horizon.
It's as if they were never there,
except I know   they were.

They were there, weren't they?
Isn't remembering   seeing? What's
        inside that inner blindness
besides a constant walking
in circles?

And yet on the street
I recognize them immediately.

A disease, a phobia,   a neurosis?

How does a face mimic
a perfectly beveled Appalachian   hilltop,
featureless,

the horse diamond without the horses?
Even though I can't see you, brother—

It's weird.
There is always a glove lying around.
Whose glove?

Does no one ever lose the pair?
It's the same as the shoes in that you never
	see both, except when they're strung
from the telephone wires.

I think the one glove is there to remind us
what we are and we aren't
to one another,

mirrors and   opposites.
Which of us is the narrative
of that other?

Sometimes I believe you're a dose
of nether serum, something that cancels out
the very meaning in things.

It's like looking into the eye of a horse.
A perfect vacancy,

a perfect oculus, a kaleidoscope of black
reminding that life is never yours
exactly, that it always belonged to

not god, but some other   totality.
Not fate.
More like accretion. No, dissipation,

a colorless, odorless,
tasteless substance.

To go to the horse diamond and look in that
animal's eye freaked me out, brother.
How it stood robot still

willing me to see more deeply,
hovering in the same
          zero gravity as the bumble bees
swarming the porch.

The bees. Brother,
I knew when I saw the wasp fly directly into
the lock of the front door
that there were such intricate
malfunctions at work, such
crude misgivings
that   the processes of remembering and
forgetting you would meld

the act of witnessing and   wonder.

It was sister who found you,
sister who investigated your sleeping so late
and called out
to us   to rush up the stairs.

So much time has passed. And hasn't.
I can't say with certainty that it ever
really happened.

I recall feeling truly holy once, brother.
Not here.
       There was a white temple
with eyes overlooking the city, monkeys
that swiped food from your hands.

The children flew kites from the tops
of derelict buildings
and the city's dirt streets.

But everyone was happy.
There was a reverence.
Pushing a bicycle tire through the alleys
was what happiness meant.

We went to the zoo
and I remember the snow leopard pacing
       the length of its cage,

agitated or nervous,   delirious or bored,

nothing but concrete and trampled earth in there.
I've learned its pace.
I learned there that most of everything
is in fact   nothing.

On the riverside, bodies transfigured into smoke
easy as dry leaves.

Most of our matter is space   unaccounted for,
emptiness, brother.

We weigh almost nil and yet we sink.

What puzzles me most though is still how
the clouds
can for a brief duration hold such an amazing
mass of rain and nothing else

(besides distillates of mood, or ideas of grandeur)

and why the steeple tops look so much more
articulate
          in rain, their sharpness
piercing the cloud cover,

why all the flowers spasm with uninhibited
sheen and glory against   grey.

Once, in the coal banks, I found a mouse
in an empty beer bottle.

It was dead, of course.   It reeked terribly
of death. I wondered
how it fit through the bottle's

aperture with no resistance on the bottle's
part.
It must have morphed itself pencil thin.

Who or what force   negotiates
these transactions?

It must have exhausted its plumb body
in a multiday attempt to
extricate itself.

That's the only way I can imagine it.
It's still a curiosity
           all this while later,
an icon of perplexity, virtuosic in self-defeat.

To find a hole in the dome of that shaft
and plunge straight down, brother, 400 feet,
that's what that's like.

Every summer we went to Black Lake
and every summer we slid the perch we caught
down the piping

that supported the dock.
I feel, not sorry, but obscenely lit with that now.

And having wasted so many birds for
practice,   in a fashion,
to understand
the life of something was to take it.

To think one could capture a glimpse
of essence escaping its   physical form in
that passing moment—
by paying close enough attention.

But you can't, brother.
You can't.

To have seen you pass from this zone
to where you are
would not help me to understand further.

We would sneak the 22° into the woods behind
the housing development,
one paved black road   leading in.

When I sighted the woodcock on the road's
shoulder, I didn't figure to miss.

I never suspected the bullet would ricochet
off the macadam's edge and careen
toward 2nd St. and 3rd.

Or later, that a woman would ask us
if we had seen anyone with a bb gun,
as she just heard
something whiz past her head.

Grandfather at night in the snow, drunk,
his too-big pants around his knees.

The bat I snared between the garage door
slamming   shut and its frame.

The stuffed wolf I have a picture of myself
sitting on in Canada.
It's as if there never was a future.

You can see it in our faces,

everyone waiting for an enthusiasm
to latch onto
among our tired dayscapes, glued

to the news, the dogs in chained orbits
around their coops,   a nouveau grotesque,
as the sunlight slowly dismantles the houses
into unforeseen hardships and

the gypsy moths
milk the trees dead dry.

The runoff comes to rest
in a clump
of twigs and garbage
and broken furniture clogging the street's grate,

Science says we are moving
at an almost impossible velocity

in multiple directions, simultaneously.
Even direction, within a large enough
reference,
           is arbitrary if not meaningless.

Sometimes   I don't feel it. At all.
Sometimes I think time
is an illusion propagated by space
in which   we were
and always will be   here.

I know this is incorrect. But I feel it.

If time is a furtherance
it is toward never knowing.

We seek to grow beyond ourselves, brother.
Even for worse.
          Is it the animal in us wanting out?
These days the animal in us, severe as it might be,
is hardly recognizable.

I often wonder if I remember things correctly.
I am convinced now that whatever force occupies
us ends up

the efflorescent pink bud
of a   dogwood,
or the vapor in an owl's call.

It's the gun chest's mahogany scent that
reminds me of you,

the neo-electrical taste of a 16 penny nail,
the delivery trucks' insecticide
fumes of derelict idle.

Science and math can't explain it. How else
can these experiences be interpreted?

If feeling isn't the equivalent   of knowing,
then what—
when I think of you and
all I can remember is trying to remember?

What are you
but a lunch-box-sized plaque in the grass now,
a period, a pinprick of ink

infinitesimal and dimensionless?

Less than.

I'd bet as hot as a star is
is as cold as you are.
I'd bet it all.

The blue jays, they call and call. The cherry
whiles in the idea of its shadow.

Is listening to the field there the same
from beneath,
like white if white could be heard?

Do you dream? Are you a dream—this one?

I cannot distinguish you from   an exhaust
trail or exhaustion.

A window, you're
blacked out.
A stairway, you keep going.

And these exchanges? Letters
to a canceled address.

Brother,   you shed us like a glacier
its stones.

If you were here,
I'd make you hold a rifle, the world magnified and
you at its scope—

I would show you the path to the river
under town.

We'd torch every abandoned vehicle
against its shore. We'd hurl rocks

in the water until
the water   changed course.

A Note on the Poem "The Resurrection Machine Mauve"

As a cento, "The Resurrection Machine Mauve" is a work of collage, borrowing words & lines from various sources in order to construct a poetic work of new breadth & meaning. This particular piece contains fragments first imagined & articulated by the following authors, in no particular order: Claudia Keelan, Luljeta Lleshanaku, John Ashbery, Laurie Sheck, Pablo Neruda, Paul Celan, Eugenio Montale, Gerald Stern, George Macbeth, Tomas Tranströmer, Kenneth Koch, Wyn Cooper, Tony Hoagland, Cesare Pavese, Billy Collins, Lynn Emanuel, Noelle Kocot, Wisława Szymborska, Anna Akhmatova, Jonathan Aaron, Jack Gilbert, Andrew Zawacki, Dean Young, Miroslav Holub, Vicente Aleixandre, Giuseppe Ungaretti, Czesław Miłosz, Galway Kinnell, Matt Hart, John Keats, Mary Ruefle, Mark Strand, Kevin Goodan, Vasko Popa, Prageeta Sharma, Donald Revell, Lucie Brock-Broido, Rainer Maria Rilke, Marie Howe, Edgar Allen Poe, Nâzım Hikmet, James Tate, W. S. Merwin, Ben Belitt, Wallace Stevens, Ada Limon, Stanley Plumly, Ralph Angel, Tadeusz Różewicz, Albert Goldbarth, David Berman, Dennis Nurkse, Milo De Angelis, René Char, Adam Zagajewski, Jen Currin, Marvin Bell, Charles Simic, Lara Glenum, Kenneth Rexroth, Martín Adán, Tomasz Różycki, Mark Cox, Amy Scattergood, Brigit Pegeen Kelly, Theodore Worozbyt, Zbigniew Herbert, Frank O'Hara, Antonio Machado, Dylan Thomas, Robert Pinsky, Aleš Debeljak, John Koethe, Donald Hall, Michael Dumanis, Andrew Kozma, Steve Scafidi, Betsy Sholl, Li-Young Lee, Linda Gregg, Richard Jackson, Mark Halliday, Fernando Pessoa. Sarah Arvio, Stan Rice, Jean Follain, Joshua Beckman, Roberto Sosa, Charles Baudelaire, Larissa Szporluk, Frank Stanford, Tomaž Šalamun, Naomi Shihab Nye, Ron Padgett, Robert Hass, Thomas Lux, Mary Karr, David Shumante, Rachel Zucker, A. R. Ammons, Aleksandar Ristovic, Edwin Arlington Robinson, Federico García Lorca, Joe Wenderoth, Novia Tadic, Richard Siken, Nicanor Parra, T. S. Eliot, Molly Peacock, Ira Sadoff, Edvard Kocbek, Peter Richards, Lance Larsen, William Olsen, James Schuyler, Philip Levine, Tryfon Tolides, William Carpenter, Robert Lowell, Baron

Wormser, Heberto Padilla, William Carlos Williams, Emily Dickinson, Dorothea Lasky, Jean-Paul Pecqueur, Richard Meier, Arthur Sze, Eugenijus Ališanka, William Matthews, Charles Wright, Andrea Baker, Tom Thompson, Jacques Roubaud, Frances Brent, Sophie Cabot Black, Forrest Gander, Tristan Tzara, James Dickey, Carrie Olivia Adams, Guillaume Apollinaire, André Breton, Robert Creeley, Sylvia Plath, Pierre Reverdy, Leslie Ullman, Lawrence Ferlinghetti, Spencer Short, C. K. Williams, Frederick Seidel, Lucy Ives, Arthur Rimbaud, & Giacomo Leopardi.

About the Poet

BILL RASMOVICZ is the author of *The World in Place of Itself* (Alice James) and *Gross Ardor* (42 Miles Press). His poems have appeared in *Hotel Amerika*, *Nimrod*, *Mid-American Review*, *Third Coast*, *Gulf Coast*, and other publications. A pharmacist, he has also served as a workshop co-leader and literary excursion leader throughout much of Europe. His current home is Brooklyn.